NATURE'S SUPERHEROES
SUPER
HUMMINGBIRDS

by Karen Latchana Kenney

pogo

Ideas for Parents and Teachers

Pogo Books let children practice reading informational text while introducing them to nonfiction features such as headings, labels, sidebars, maps, and diagrams, as well as a table of contents, glossary, and index.

Carefully leveled text with a strong photo match offers early fluent readers the support they need to succeed.

Before Reading

- "Walk" through the book and point out the various nonfiction features. Ask the student what purpose each feature serves.
- Look at the glossary together. Read and discuss the words.

Read the Book

- Have the child read the book independently.
- Invite him or her to list questions that arise from reading.

After Reading

- Discuss the child's questions. Talk about how he or she might find answers to those questions.
- Prompt the child to think more. Ask: What did you know about hummingbirds before you read this book? What more do you want to learn after reading it?

Pogo Books are published by Jump!
5357 Penn Avenue South
Minneapolis, MN 55419
www.jumplibrary.com

Library of Congress Cataloging-in-Publication Data

Names: Kenney, Karen Latchana, author.
Title: Super hummingbirds / by Karen Latchana Kenney.
Description: Minneapolis, MN: Jump!, Inc., [2018]
Series: Nature's superheroes | Audience: Ages 7–10.
Includes bibliographical references and index.
Identifiers: LCCN 2017031318 (print)
LCCN 2017031515 (ebook)
ISBN 9781624967092 (ebook)
ISBN 9781620319710 (hardcover: alk. paper)
ISBN 9781620319727 (pbk.)
Subjects: LCSH: Hummingbirds—Juvenile literature.
Classification: LCC QL696.A558 (ebook) | LCC QL696.
A558 K46 2017 (print) | DDC 598.7/64—dc23
LC record available at https://lccn.loc.gov/2017031318

Editor: Jenna Trnka
Book Designer: Michelle Sonnek
Photo Researcher: Michelle Sonnek

Photo Credits: Mike Truchon/Shutterstock, cover (bird), 1 (flowers), 23; Lepas/Shutterstock, cover (flowers); StevenRussellSmithPhotos/Shutterstock, 1 (bird); Kenneth Canning/iStock, 3; BirdImages/iStock, 4; Jack Milchanowski/Alamy, 5; Wang LiQiang/Shutterstock, 6-7; Corbis/Getty, 8; Tim Zurowski/Shutterstock, 9; Ondrej Prosicky/Shutterstock, 10-11; Warren Price Photography/Shutterstock, 12-13; Birdiegal/Shutterstock, 14-15; Matt Cuda/Shutterstock, 16; KEVIN ELSBY/Alamy, 17; zhuclear/iStock, 18-19; Steve Shinn/Alamy, 20-21.

Printed in the United States of America at Corporate Graphics in North Mankato, Minnesota.

TABLE OF CONTENTS

CHAPTER 1

TINY BIRDS

What bird can fly backward and **hover** in the air like a helicopter? And what bird can flap its wings faster than any other bird?

It is tiny. It is super fast. And it has some amazing powers. It is a hummingbird!

There are more than 330 kinds of hummingbirds. Many weigh less than a penny! The tiniest is also the smallest bird in the world. It is the bee hummingbird.

DID YOU KNOW?

A bee hummingbird's eggs are the size of coffee beans. Its nest is the size of a quarter.

CHAPTER 2

SUPERHERO POWERS

All birds can fly forward. But only hummingbirds can fly backward. They can also fly up, down, and hover in one spot. They even fly upside down!

To hover, a hummingbird moves its wings in a certain way. They don't flap up and down. They move forward and backward in a figure eight shape.

Hummingbirds are strong and fast. Some beat their wings 80 times in one second! Their wings flap so hard it creates a buzzing noise or hum. This is what gives these birds their name.

DID YOU KNOW?

Hummingbirds don't use their feet to walk or even hop. They only use them to **perch** and give their wings a rest.

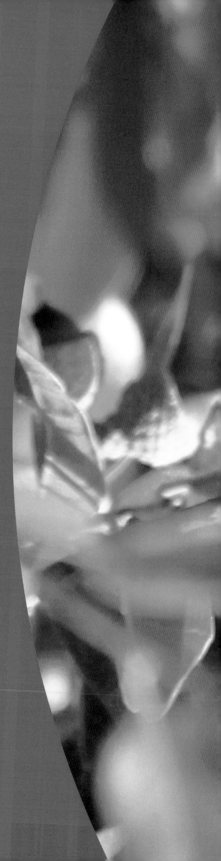

Hummingbirds are able to go into **torpor**. They hang from a branch in a deep sleep. This helps them stay alive and save **energy** when it is cold outside. Then the bird wakes itself up when the weather is warm again.

One of the hummingbird's best powers is its sharp eyesight. These fast fliers need to see well. It helps them avoid crashing into trees and other birds.

Good eyesight also helps hummingbirds catch fast insects. Once they spot one, they fly in close. Then they snap their beaks shut over the bug.

CHAPTER 3
FUELED BY FLOWERS

Where do hummingbirds get fuel for their powers? Flowers! They can hover right in front of them. Their long beaks and tongues reach hidden **nectar**.

Some hummingbird beaks perfectly fit certain flowers. One is the sword-billed hummingbird. Its beak is longer than its body. It feeds on long flowers. It reaches nectar other birds can't reach.

Hummingbirds eat nectar from flowers. Their long, skinny tongues have **grooves**. These grooves help pull nectar out. The sweet liquid gives the birds lots of energy to fly.

tongue

TAKE A LOOK!

A hummingbird has many features that make it one of nature's superheroes!

WINGS
Wings beat fast to help a hummingbird hover in front of flowers.

EYE
Eyes with sharp eyesight help the bird fly and find insects.

TONGUE
A tongue with grooves pulls nectar out of flowers.

BEAK
A long, narrow beak reaches far into flowers.

FEET
Feet grip tree branches when resting or in torpor.

Hummingbirds and flowers help each other. **Pollen** gets stuck on hummingbirds while they eat. They visit other flowers and leave some pollen behind. This helps the plants make seeds. Soon new plants grow.

Hummingbirds dart from flower to flower. Their powers help them find the fuel they need to fly fast. Can you spot one? Can you hear it hum?

pollen

ACTIVITIES & TOOLS

MAKE A HUMMINGBIRD FEEDER

Make a feeder and watch hummingbirds feed in your yard.

What You Need:

- baby food jar
- nail
- red tape
- wire
- water
- sugar
- spoon
- measuring cup
- notebook
- pencil

❶ Stick red tape on the lid. Hummingbirds like the color red.

❷ Ask an adult for help with steps 2 and 3. Use the nail to poke a hole in the lid of the baby food jar.

❸ Make nectar from the sugar and water. Mix ½ cup (118 milliliters) sugar with 1 cup (237 mL) boiling water. Mix until the sugar dissolves. Then mix in 1 cup (237 mL) of cold water.

❹ Fill the baby food jar with the nectar. Screw on the lid.

❺ Attach a wire loop around the lid. Ask an adult for help, if needed.

❻ Hang the feeder outside by a window. Make sure to add more nectar each day.

❼ Watch the feeder in the mornings. Do you see any hummingbirds? Write down what you see in your notebook.

❽ Look over your notes after a few days. What is the same each day? What is different?

GLOSSARY

energy: The strength to be active and move around without getting tired.

grooves: Long cuts on the surface of something.

hover: To stay in one place in the air.

nectar: A sweet liquid in flowers that birds and insects drink.

perch: To rest on a perch, such as a branch.

pollen: Tiny yellow grains made by flowers.

torpor: A state of being inactive.

INDEX

TO LEARN MORE

Learning more is as easy as 1, 2, 3.

1) Go to www.factsurfer.com

2) Enter "superhummingbirds" into the search box.

3) Click the "Surf" button to see a list of websites.

With factsurfer, finding more information is just a click away.